Solo

Monologues for Drama in English

JOHN GOODWIN
and BILL TAYLOR

Hodder & Stoughton

A MEMBER OF THE HODDER HEADLINE GROUP

Acknowledgements

Many people have helped in the preparation of this book and the authors are indebted to them all. In particular we would like to thank the following:
Vicki Bennett for *Molly*; Charlotte Ellen for *Grace* and *Adrian*; Selwyn Hawtin for material relating to the *Titanic* collection of monologues; Jake Oldershaw for *Dom*, *Lara*, and *Mr Hardy*; and Karen Young for *Gillian*.

Orders: Please contact Bookpoint Ltd, 130 Milton Park, Abingdon, Oxon OX14 4SB. Telephone: (44) 01235 827720, Fax: (44) 01235 400454. Lines are open from 9 am – 6 pm Monday to Saturday, with a 24-hour message answering service. Email address: orders@bookpoint.co.uk

British Library Cataloguing in Publication Data
A catalogue record for this title is available from The British Library

ISBN 0-340-655283

First published 1996
Impression number   10 9 8 7 6 5 4 3
Year   2005 2004 2003 2002 2001

Copyright © 1996

Typeset by Wearset, Bolden, Tyne and Wear.
Printed in Great Britain for Hodder & Stoughton Educational, a division of Hodder Headline Plc, 338 Euston Road, London NW1 3BH by The Bath Press, Bath

Contents

1 BIRTH

2 BIRTH AND DEATH

3 LOVE

4 DEATH

5 DEATH ROW

6 MONOLOGUES IN ACTION

Introduction

This collection of monologues provides starting points for work in Drama, English and Personal and Social Education. They are designed for study at Key Stage 4 and offer moral dilemmas which can be explored through discussion, practical drama work, written work and a variety of active learning strategies. All the monologues are based on fictional characters even though some explore real events. There is a range of material here from the contemporary to the historical, from humorous to serious, and a number of interrelated monologues offering differing and contrasting viewpoints. All are accessible and of interest to young people.

The book also includes a section entitled 'Monologues in Action' in which strategies for exploring and further extending the monologues are suggested. These strategies involve students:

- reading the text individually and in groups
- listening to and talking about the issues raised, and challenging or developing attitudes and values
- telling stories from different points of view. A story relating to a particular monologue is retold in the voice of characters other than the one in the monologue. This can be done in pairs or small groups and presented in spoken or written form
- writing new monologues to challenge or support the views of the monologues in the book
- taking the 'hot seat' to answer questions in role in order to provide information or to highlight feelings and emotions
- image making, creating still images to represent key moments in the fictional life of characters or an image of past or future events
- in Forum Theatre replaying moments of difficult interaction in the lives of any of the characters, taking time out to suggest alternative ways of overcoming the difficulties

- writing in role
- outlining a character in a monologue. Drawing a large outline of a character and asking the class to fill the outline with appropriate written thoughts, feelings or things said and done by the character
- writing letters, diaries or notes as written by, or between, the characters.

These strategies will generate ideas so that pupils and teachers can select appropriate and practical ways of exploring the fictional material.

About the authors

John Goodwin and Bill Taylor, writers of award-winning drama scripts for BBC Radio, now provide this third collection of monologues in the *Solo* series, published by Hodder and Stoughton. *Solo 1* and *Solo 2*, which have reprinted many times already, are now available in new updated editions.

Interrelated monologues are indicated in the Contents, e.g.

Terry }
Beth   }

1 *Birth*

Terry

(Terry has just become a father for the first time.)

Hospital corridor, six o'clock in the morning. No sleep. No breakfast. Can't even get a morning paper. But I'm not complaining because today is a special sort of day . . . a day I'll always remember. Today I became a dad. Mother and baby are fine, both fast asleep.

It's me that's feeling a bit shaky. I was there for the birth. I didn't think I could go through with it . . . but I managed. Luckily it all happened very quickly.

Sitting here these few minutes I've had chance to recover a bit and time to wonder. To ask myself what kind of dad I'm going to be for baby Laura. I had two dads . . . not at the same time of course . . . and they were both useless. So I just hope I make a better job of it than they did.

Beth

(Beth has recently given birth to a baby and is the partner of Terry.)

Baby Laura is perfect. She seems so happy and contented. It's just Terry that's the problem. I think he's beginning to crack up. Before the birth he was so fussy. He wouldn't let me do anything. He insisted I gave up work and read book after book about what we should do during my pregnancy and when the baby was born. He decorated the spare bedroom, bought piles of toys and baby clothes. He even put a deposit down on a baby bike for her.

'This is crazy, Terry,' I said. 'It will be years before she'll want to ride a bike.'

'I don't care,' he said. 'I want our baby to have the best.'
Now she's born it's much worse. He stands by her cot for hours and at night he lies awake listening for any slight sound that might come from her room.

I know he means well but I'm exhausted by his worrying. I just wish he'd relax.

Gemma

(Gemma has very recently become involved with a fundamental religious group.)

Something has happened to me. I have been reborn. It is absolutely amazing. It's as if I'm seeing the world anew and discovering everything for the first time. Suddenly my life has new meaning. It all happened so quickly. Only last week I was in town and I met Greg. Greg was reborn five years ago and now spends all his time working for salvation. He was giving out leaflets and asked me if I wanted to visit their church. He had such a smiling face, I couldn't say no.

Their church is the old tin shack at the end of the road where I live. The old tin shack with flaking paint, a rusty roof and broken windows. That is on the outside. But inside it was so different. Greg told me it would be. Inside it's so bright and alive.

I didn't know what to expect the first time. But it is so beautiful. The singing and chanting and clapping and swaying with all those people is wonderful.

'Hallelujah,' we cry. 'Hallelujah For The Eternal One. Praise for our life. Praise for our souls.'

We are all so happy. The whole building pulsates with our love. The floor bounces to our stamping and dancing and chanting. For the first time in my life I am alive. Hallelujah.

Emma

(Emma has been Gemma's friend since they both went to primary school together.)

I can't believe it. I keep telling myself it's a phase she's going through and that very soon she'll see what a sham it is. She tried to get me to go with her, to that tin shack with the broken windows. I said, 'No way.' Mum says a load of weirdos have bought the place and that I should stay away. So that's exactly what I intend to do.

But not Gemma. Oh no, not Gemma. It's so unlike her to get mixed up with trouble. Now she's down there every night. After school, every night. Yesterday she turned on me and started to pull at the silver chain I wear round my neck. Her fingers gripped the tiny silver zodiac sign on the middle of the chain. I thought she was going to choke me to death. I've never seen her like that before. Then she cries out, 'This is the devil's toy. It's putting you in the power of Satan.'

She wouldn't let go till she'd broken the chain and thrown it to the ground. Oh Gemma, what is happening to you?

Erna

(Erna lived in Germany during the Second World War and remembers the time she gave birth to her baby on the bare earth.)

We were bombed by British planes in January 1945. My house was completely destroyed but my life and those of my two young children were saved by fleeing to the air raid shelters just as the blitz began. We could not return to our house which was now no more than a pile of dust and rubble and we had to be evacuated to a farm out of the city. My youngest child and I had to sleep in a wooden shed and the eldest had to make do with a pig sty for his bedroom.

Whilst we were there a huge bomb fell very close to the farm. It was like a terrible nightmare and it was a miracle that we were not all killed. But we had to be evacuated again. It was in the middle of winter and the Allied troops were closing in around us as we made our way to our new destination. That night the British started very heavy shelling of the area and our way ahead was blocked by fallen trees. Suddenly my labour pains started. There were no doctors or midwives with us, in fact no trained help at all. I gave birth to my new baby on the bare earth in a field. My only helper was a woman who lit a candle by us and stayed with me for some time. Who she was, and where she went, I will never know. She saw to the delivery of my baby and then disappeared and I never saw her again.

Grace

(Grace remembers a visit to one of her relatives when she was quite young.)

It was mainly Sundays. Visiting car days; days upon days without the rain to relieve us. The miles trudged on in that family car, we were packed in so tight. Sign and sight of the familiar lane ahead as we would ask, 'Are we nearly there yet?' They would answer, 'Not long now'.

Along the end of the familiar lane I'd ask myself, how many times at this place? Replace, relocate. The hall was for greeting, kettle ready boiled and cups waiting, touch comfortably in appropriate places. The family house was tired and all lay fretful on the shelf; time and date unchanged; 3.30 July 12, no year stated. Then it was into the garden. Life breathed there still, then wrapped up for next time. Put away in that shed till next time, end time, forgotten time.

That spring the offspring announced their news. It came in a tattered card and out of the stork's mouth came a bubble which read,

'It's a boy.'

Opened, it revealed the new family member was to be known as Edward. I imagined a tweed jacket, flat cap and Hamlet cigar. But the image was replaced when already 'Oooh . . . Aaah' sounds were falling upon my ears. The sight of the new one is still imprinted upon my memory. So tiny. Thin skin with pulsating heart inside, flickering eyes and bubbly mouth. Are you real?

Without asking or waiting for an answer I lifted the child from the sticky pink blanket and held him in my arms. So light and afraid to the stranger's touch but opening absent eyes he smiled. Grasping hands reached and stretched. A delicate finger pointed towards the window and out over prospect field.

Crystal

(Crystal is 19 years old. She has just given birth to Ryan.)

Look at him. His tiny little hands, his tiny little toes. I've never felt so happy. I could sit here forever, holding him in my arms. He's so tiny.

I wonder how he'll grow up. He's only a few days old but even now you can tell things about him. He's strong and restless, like he can't wait to grow up and get on with his life. He always wants to know what's going on. He doesn't sleep as much as most new born babies do.

The nurses say he's going to be a right little handful. I don't care. He's my baby, he's a little part of me. Whatever he's like I know I'll always love him.

Dom

(Dom is 22 and is a DJ in 'Heaven'.)

Yeah wicked, it was huge man, I'm tellin' ya. The place was heavin'. My name was up there on all the flyers an' everythin'. Well, not my real name of course, that's not cool. My tag? 'DJ Birth'. Yeah, I know it sounds a bit cheesy but it's what it stands for, man. 'BIRTH', 'A New Generation', 'Music for the Future'. It could be big I'm tellin' ya. Yeah well I know I'm only third on the bill, but there's some champion DJ's y'know? 'Grooverider', 'Top Cat' . . . You've gotta make your way slow. Prove yourself. But I know so long as I keep droppin' my own tunes in my own style, I'll get there. Then it'll be big up to the Birth Posse all over the country, man. Even Europe! I'll even be able to make my own tunes soon as I get paid an' get my own equipment. It's all there waiting for me.

Lara

(Lara is 18 and has seen 'DJ Birth' play.)

Me and some mates went to 'Heaven' last night. It was amazing. Soon as we got in we were split up. I didn't see them all night, but did it matter? Three main floors spinning House, Trance and Jungle with Chill Out rooms and a Dub shack. I stayed in the Jungle Room mostly. There was this brilliant DJ, 'Birth' I think, though I couldn't really tell 'cos he was behind all these machines. As soon as I stepped in the room the rhythm took over. It was like another world! Everyone smiling, dancing, sweating. Nobody cared! I've never felt so comfortable with people I didn't know before. It was such a different experience. I don't understand why people need drugs when they go out clubbing. I mean, I was *so* happy and all I had was water all night. I don't think many do take them anymore. I'll go and see 'DJ Birth' again. It's changed my life.

Mr Hardy

(Mr Hardy is Dom's dad.)

He used to be such a quiet boy. He used to make me
proud. I could sleep safe at night knowing he was home,
maybe working for school the next day, maybe enjoying
watching the television. That all changed when he went to
college. I remember it vividly. He worked so hard to get
there. Started going to those rave things, didn't he? Started
staying up all night dancing, 'high' on some brain melting
drug, no doubt. I mean I can understand a few drinks
down the pub, but why do they do it? Well, it took over his
life didn't it? Just like the paper said it would. Gave up
college. Wanted to be a . . . DJ . . . or whatever they call it.
It was as if he were a new person. He got himself on the
dole, I saw him less and less, hardly recognised him. I mean
my own son! I told him, I said you go straight back to
college and give up that rubbish or I never want to see you
again. When I was a kid I respected my parents, did what
they asked. Kids. They just cause problems.

2 *Birth and Death*

Titanic *was magnificent. The ship was the largest man-made moving object that had ever been built. More than 11,300 shipyard workers had built and fitted the vessel and many claimed the ship was 'unsinkable'. Many of the 2,238 passengers who sailed on the ship's maiden voyage in 1912 were emigrating to begin a new life in America.*

At midnight April 14, two days into the maiden voyage, the ship hit an iceberg and sank. Only 705 passengers Survived. Seventy years later the wreck of Titanic *was discovered lying on the sea bed. Since then objects and belongings of those who died when the ship sank have been brought to the surface and placed in a museum.*

This collection of monologues is based on these facts but uses fictional characters.

Henry Stone

(Henry Stone was aboard Titanic *for her sea trials on April 2, 1912, to report for his magazine* The Engineer.*)*

Fine today; calm. The tugs arrived just after 6 am and had us mid-channel in hardly any time. Huge crowds turned out to see us; must have been hundreds of them and you should have heard the cheers. But then, she must have looked a wonderful sight in the rising sun. Black hull, white painted superstructure, and that thin gold line running the whole 800 feet – every inch of her 'White Star' and proud of it! But the real glory – I'll never forget it! – a few miles out to sea and the tugs had cast off, we almost held our breath! The order from the bridge, a short burst of bells, a sort of throb running through the vessel, and with the gentlest of shudders she was under way. The mammoth, the leviathan, *Titanic* was under her own steam.

Lunch was in the dining room. I could hardly eat for excitement. All around me was luxury and splendour and hardly a ripple disturbed the surface of my soup. We might have been ashore in a first class hotel.

During the afternoon *Titanic* made nearly 21 knots with scarcely a tremor and underwent emergency tests, stopping in a little under half a mile. The Board of Trade Inspector seemed well satisfied when we got home just after 7 pm, as well he might. He won't see the like of this magnificent vessel again.

Alice

(Alice, a survivor of the Titanic, *was 19 years old when it sank.)*

Oh, I can remember lots. Who could ever forget that night? We were on our way to America to start a new life. My parents, my young brother, and me.

My father kept saying, 'It's the birth of something better for us'. I don't know how many times he said that but I know he believed it with all his heart.

It was so cold. A kind of cold that still gnaws my bones and won't go away. The saloon of the ship was full to bursting. Young children under everybody's feet. And laughter. Laughter and singing with somebody playing the piano. Then that collision with the iceberg and nobody believing we could come to any harm. The ship was supposed to be unsinkable, that's what everybody kept saying, and they went on with their laughing and singing.

I don't remember what happened next only that I was in a lifeboat with children crying all around me. Young Arthur, my brother, was lying slumped over my waist and he felt so very heavy. We were shivering with the cold and all the time we could see that great ship sticking out of the water at a crazy angle until her propeller was clear of the water. Then the lights went out on the ship and everything was black.

My father never did get to America and my young brother died in the lifeboat, slumped across my waist. It was not the birth of something better for us, only the beginning of a cold night that won't go away.

Howard Coyne

(Howard is head of a corporation which finances large scale projects.)

Straight away, I got on the phone. I had to make that guy an offer! He'd made a discovery the world had been waiting half a century for. The wreck of the *Titanic*! Now, let me think, the *Titanic* sank sometime before the war, I guess. They'll pay millions to see all that stuff from the wreck. Can't you just picture it? 'Toy – clutched by child as ship went down after head on collision!' Anyway, that guy's going to need cash, and it's going to be me that gives it to him. Of course, the honour of finding the *Titanic* will still be his, but it's going to be my name people think of when they see all that junk brought up from the ocean bed. And there's all those stories about gold bullion! In any case, those millionaires must have had loads of gems, gold watches, and valuables on them when they went to the bottom. We're going to be rich, but rich!

Ted Weaver

(Ted was one of the American crew on the expedition searching for the wreck of the Titanic.*)*

I can understand how easy it is to lose all sense of direction in the Sahara. The ocean bed was just as big and deserted and scanning it day after day was just as monotonous. Damn it, the wreck had to be there somewhere. No-one had moved it! I guess that's what kept us staring at that empty video screen, hour after hour. In fact, we'd all but given up. Perhaps that's why I found it hard to believe that small, round, half-buried object was what we were looking for.

We're back! And this time we've got some real sophisticated equipment. The secrets of the *Titanic* are coming to the surface courtesy of a deep-water sub and a camera that goes where no-one's been since 1912. I can hardly wait to see what she looks like when the sub comes in at the prow.

Unbelievable! It takes your breath away. Even with the railings mangled, you can see how beautiful she was. Maybe this is how *Titanic*'s builders felt seventy years ago. That's the foremast lying askew the bridge, so that must be the crow's nest. Think of those poor guys freezing their socks off up there and suddenly seeing that iceberg, 800 yards ahead. I guess they didn't know they were a few yards too late and that was the ship's doom coming towards them at 21 knots!

Yep! I'm shouting, along with the rest. I've been there and seen it – the glory of the *Titanic* not faded, sea-changed.

Marjorie

(Marjorie lives in Welwyn Garden City with her husband.)

We mostly enjoy documentaries, but this was such a shock. George, my husband could see it was upsetting me, so he put his paper down and sat on the arm of my chair. 'We can switch it off you know,' he said. But I felt I had to know what it was all about. Of course, it's marvellous what they can do today, pictures from miles under the sea, cameras searching, probing. Prying I call it. We faced it together, George holding my hand, supporting. You see, this was Daddy's resting place they were plundering. Unsinkable, they called it and there weren't enough lifeboats you know. So my father died along with all the others, pulled to the bottom with the *Titanic* and everything in it. And now they're bringing things up to be stared at in a museum. It all came straight back, Mummy and me, ever so proud, waving him off, and Daddy at the rail smiling. She never got over it you know; never even saw the Armistice. And now they're robbing his grave. I thought I'd finished suffering.

Lokiath

(Lokiath is a young person who lives under the shadow of the mountains.)

I was up early, when it was just getting light. Cold morning. Saw the sun rising and shining on the snow. No breakfast, in fact, nothing to eat at all. Went outside. It was so quiet. There was just me.

Then I saw it . . . right outside my house . . . and Verun's house. It was pressed into the snow. There is no mistake. It is the footprint. The footprint we have all been dreading to find.

Maslov

(Maslov is an elder of the people who live under the shadow of the mountains.)

There is an old legend of the people who live under the shadow of the mountains. The old legend is almost as ancient as the mountains themselves. It tells us how a great and terrible creature once destroyed the village where our people lived. It destroyed their houses and took many lives.

Those who were not killed fled the village and came to this place. Here we have lived in peace for many generations.

Two moons ago there was thunder in the mountains. It was a kind of thunder that has not been heard before . . . that is except once. This thunder means the birth of a new terrible creature. We all know that in our hearts. Next will come the giant footprint in the snow. It is only a matter of time. When we see that, it will be the sign that the creature has truly been born. With its birth there will be deaths in our village. The legend is a curse that we can't escape.

Ravi

(Ravi has become a leader of a group of local people who are opposed to the building of the dam and is on his way to the site along with thousands of others in order to disrupt the work.)

I have dreamed of making this journey for ages. In my dream I travelled alone. But as I travel today many thousands of people share the road with me. On this journey we are all friends together. We are friends with the same purpose.

Amongst us are those who have lost their homes and villages as the waters rise behind this terrible wall. Families have been divided. Nobody has been given proper compensation. Those that refused to leave have had their homes seized and they have been carried off in lorries in the middle of the night.

Holy rivers have been diverted and contaminated. Villages have died because the wells that were once fed by these rivers are now dry. There is no respect for our way of life, for our customs and traditions. Only one thing matters now. It is greed for money by those who build this dam. Money is the new god.

So we march to stop the building. We do not come in violence. But this work has to stop. If we have to lie down in front of the trucks to stop the work then that is what we will do. Those who drive the trucks will see the error of what is happening. Then they will stop their work and come to join us and that will be an end of this dam.

Simon

(Simon is a director of a British engineering company and is directing the building of a huge new dam in India.)

I have dreamed of a project like this for years. It is a chance to make my mark on the world. The new dam is the birth of a new way of life for so many people in this part of India. It will bring electricity to many villages for the very first time. There will be an endless supply of clean drinking water to the whole region and a chance to end disease and famine. It will also of course give our company an international reputation of the very highest calibre. It is the dawn of a new age for us all.

I have to admit that with some local Indian people the project is not very popular. But they are a tiny minority. Some hot heads are trying to cause disruption to the building work. It is to be expected, but it's not a problem. When the region realises the enormous benefit this project will bring them, they will be grateful for all our efforts on their behalf.

3 *Love*

Michael

(14 years old.)

I love her. She's beautiful. She's the most beautiful person I've ever met. She's got the bluest eyes I've ever seen. And the blondest hair. And the nicest teeth. She hasn't got any fillings. I love the way she smiles.

She lives in a house by the park. She hasn't got any brothers or sisters. Sometimes her dad gives her a lift to school, but mostly she walks through the park with her friends. She's got loads of friends. I want to tell her how much I love her but I can never get near her.

I nearly spoke to her once. I was standing behind her in the dinner queue and it would've been dead easy to tap her on the shoulder, but I couldn't think what to say, not with hundreds of prying eyes staring at me. And I don't think she was in a good mood because when I reached past her to get at the chocolate chip cookies she frowned and said, 'Do you mind? There's a queue you know'.

One day I'll tell her how I feel. Maybe I'll see her in the park, on her own.

Trevor says I only fancy her because she's good looking, but that's not why I love her. I love her because . . . well, it's hard to say really. She's not like other people. She's, sort of, perfect. If she was mine I'd be happy forever.

Joanna

(14 years old.)

God, why won't he go away? Everywhere I turn, there he is. He pretends I can't see him. He looks the other way, or ties up his shoelaces, or just walks past me with an embarrassed expression on his face.

It's getting worse. He's started following me home. Some nights when I'm walking in the park I can hear footsteps behind me, and when I turn round I catch him jumping behind a bush. The first time it happened I was dead scared – I thought I was being followed by some weirdo – but once I'd realised it was only Michael I just felt annoyed. Why is he doing this? He must have twigged by now that I'm not interested.

One time he stood right behind me in the dinner queue. I could feel him brushing against me. I got dead stroppy and told him to stop pestering me. But he must be stupid or something because that very evening there he was again hiding under a hedge.

I don't want to make a fuss. My friends think it's a great laugh. I know he wouldn't hurt me, he's as soft as a bad tooth. I don't want to hurt his feelings. I just wish there was a simple way of getting him to leave me alone.

Pat

(15 years old.)

I love Sam. I love Sam with all my heart. No one has ever meant so much to me. No one else ever will. Sometimes you KNOW. You look at someone and you know that this is the person you're going to spend the rest of your life with.

We're always together. We go to the same school. We're in the same class. We do the same options. We live a few streets apart. We've always been friends but now it's much more than that. I couldn't imagine not being with Sam.

So why is everyone making such a big fuss? Why are Sam's parents trying to drive us apart? Why do people snigger behind our backs? Is love a crime?

'Romeo'

(17 years old.)

I can't tell you my real name. It's too dangerous.

I've been seeing 'Juliet' for nearly a year. (That's not her real name either.) We have a place where we meet. I can't tell you where it is. We've made it into a bit of a retreat. There's a camping stove that I picked up second hand, and an old kettle and a couple of chipped mugs, and a tin for some biscuits. There isn't any furniture, just a few old cushions, and the place stinks a bit, but at least it's ours. At least we're safe there.

Usually we see each other a couple of times a week. Juliet tells her family that she's staying late after school, or she's going to the library. That way we can meet up for an hour or so without anyone getting suspicious.

So far it's worked out quite well. But I wish we didn't have to be like this. I want to tell people about us, but I know I can't. My dad would have a fit if he knew who I was seeing. And Juliet's parents are no better. They're trying to force her to marry one of her cousins.

I've decided there's only one solution to this problem. We'll have to run away. I've packed a few things and I've got a couple of hundred pounds saved. Juliet's due here any minute now. Then we'll be away for good. We'll get married. It's our lives, after all.

'Juliet'

(17 years old.)

What am I going to do? I'm too young to get married.

It's not that I don't like Rashid. We've always got on well. My mother says I'm very lucky. Some men are domineering and want to boss you about but Rashid's not like that at all. He's very polite and considerate.

Maybe I should marry him. I'm sure we'd be quite happy together. He agrees that I should finish school and go to college. In many ways he's very modern in his thinking. Rashid says that if you live in two worlds at once you must make compromises, that way everyone's happy. But marrying him would be like living with your best friend. I don't love Rashid. I love 'Romeo'.

Sometimes I feel like standing up for myself and telling my parents all about my secret boyfriend. I know they'd try to stop me seeing him, but I'm sure that in the end they'd come to terms with it. They'd have to.

But then I think about Romeo's dad. He runs the local newsagents. Whenever I go in there he looks at me like I'm dirt. There's a lot of people like that around here. Romeo's dad would never accept me. More importantly, I wouldn't want him to. People like that make me sick. I love Romeo but I don't want to be part of his family.

Romeo talks about running away. But why should we? There must be another way of sorting things out.

Julie

(Julie is in her early twenties, married, with a small child.)

I bumped into Steve at Tesco's. We hadn't seen each other since school. And then, suddenly, there he was, in between the dry pasta and the tinned tomatoes. We stood chatting for ages. Steve was my first-ever boyfriend and we had a lot of news to catch up on. 'What you doing on Wednesday?' he asked. 'Nothing much,' I told him. Nothing that can't be videoed for later. 'OK, then,' he said, 'I'll take you down Roxanne's'.

I thought, why not? I deserved a night on the town. Nick was away again. He's often away during the week, at some sales conference or regional promotion. Meanwhile, I'm left at home, holding the baby. Just because I'm married doesn't mean I can't go out and enjoy myself once in a while, does it?

We had a great time at Roxanne's. I'd forgotten how Steve could make me laugh. I'd always felt special with Steve. He's got a sort of, sparkle. Something alive. Something dangerous. He knows how to enjoy himself. Nick's idea of a good time is watching Jeremy Beadle.

We danced all night. Then at the end, during the slow number, somehow we ended up kissing. I knew it was wrong but I couldn't help myself. For the first time in ages I really felt wanted.

Steve invited me back to his place. I told him I couldn't possibly do that. After all, I'm a married woman. But then we kissed again and somehow that didn't seem to matter anymore.

I phoned the baby sitter and asked her if she minded sleeping over. I decided, right, if she objects to me staying out, that's it, I'll go straight home and forget about Steve completely. But she was glad of the extra money.

Well, I thought as I got into Steve's car, once won't hurt, will it? As long as Nick doesn't find out.

Molly

(Molly is considering the failure of her marriage.)

I always thought I'd feel really special when I got married
. . . a Cinderella bride, blushing beautiful down the aisle
with my Prince Charming by my side. It didn't turn out like
that at all. I stood in a disgusting room in front of a woman
rattling on about 'the solemn nature of marriage' and a kid
behind me screaming 'I want a wee . . . I want a wee,' and I
didn't feel beautiful at all. I just felt stupid and overdressed.

I wanted to run and cry out, 'I can't do it'. Couldn't they
all see the frightened little girl inside me? What was I
thinking of? All those smiling people, telling me 'fairy tales
do happen'. Who was I to disappoint them?

No one tries to find me now. The blushing bride is soon
forgotten when she becomes the battered wife. No one
wants to see the bruised limbs or swollen face. Those that
do see find it easier to believe that I've had a run-in with
another door with psychopathic anti-social tendencies than
to believe me when I say married bliss isn't all it's cracked
up to be. Sometimes lying is a less bitter pill to swallow
than the truth.

He speaks of other things. Like DIY and football and 'why
isn't the dinner ready?' and 'the place is in a mess,' and
'*somebody* didn't clean it up'. But most of all he says when
will I start to learn to behave like a real wife should? I cry
into the sink. I want to ask him how can we go on like this.
He says, 'make the tea . . . let's pretend . . . let's play
mummies and daddies, happy together.'

Over the radio the love songs play on.

Lydia

(17 years old.)

The first time was a bit of a disaster. I suppose we were both a bit nervous. Robbie was paranoid about his mum getting home and catching us, which was a bit of an over-reaction since she was two hundred miles away visiting his auntie. It was silly really, especially when you think of the things we got up to when his mum was downstairs watching telly. But I suppose when you finally decide you're going all the way it changes things.

Turning the lights out was a mistake. All that fumbling around in the darkness. And Robbie pretending he knew what he was doing didn't help much. I was expecting something grand and earth shattering and in the end we just, well, did it. It just happened. I remember thinking, 'This isn't how it's meant to be, surely? We'll have to try again'.

The next time was a big improvement. We kept the lights on. We felt much more relaxed being able to see each other. It was much more of a sharing thing. And that's what sex is about, isn't it? Sharing your love.

Now when we have sex I feel really close to Robbie. I feel that we really love each other. Of course, we're careful. You have to be nowadays with HIV and AIDS and what have you. After all, loving someone doesn't mean you want to take risks or get pregnant!

Robbie

(17 years old.)

The first time was amazing. I felt a bit awkward to begin with, worrying about whether it would be OK and half expecting Lydia to change her mind at the last moment, but once we were under the covers it just sort of, well, happened. It was sort of automatic, like nature taking over.

I think Lydia enjoyed it too. Well, she must have, because we have done it lots of times since. Now we do it with the lights on!
I'd been out with a few girls before Lydia but none of them wanted to have sex. I was beginning to worry there was something wrong with me. Lydia's helped me prove there isn't.

I'm very careful. I always use a condom. I like Lydia a lot, but I don't want to get her pregnant. There's a whole new world out there waiting to be discovered.

Ben

(Ben is 17 and has just heard his father threaten his mother.)

I knew it was getting worse. They've been at each other's throats for weeks. There were the long silences at meal times when they wouldn't even look at each other. I've become a salt and pepper, sugar, and tomato sauce go-between at a table of hate. 'Ask your father to pass me that knife, Ben. That is unless he needs two knives and two forks to shovel his food down his throat.'

'Tell your mother, Ben, that if she wants a knife and fork she should have used her brains and put them by her plate before we began to eat the meal.'

Our house has become a big tennis match with both of them trying to score points off each other and I'm expected to be the umpire. A backhand winner for sarcasm followed by a volley of frosty silence, then an over-the-net shot of obstinacy and a serve of sheer abuse. Forty love is the score.

Only there's no love any more. Just warfare and attrition and I know something very nasty is going to happen very soon. My mother started an Open University degree course and my dad just can't cope. She's due to go off to summer school next month but he wants us to go on holiday like we do every year.

Last night the meal time skirmishes broke out into full-scale war.

'If you go, I shall burn all your books,' he said. 'All your study stuff, books, papers and junk will be on the bonfire'. There was a long silence and then my mother said coldly, 'You wouldn't dare. Because if you did I would never let you back in this house. I'd change all the locks and you'd never get back in'.

Sometimes it's been very funny, this tennis match tussle. But not any more. Now it's scary and I just don't know what to do.

Tim

(Tim is Ben's father.)

Oh, dear. I got it wrong. Very, very wrong. I shouldn't have said it. I know it was one big mistake. The words were out of my mouth and on my lips before I knew what I'd said. I don't mean it. Of course I'd never burn her books or destroy her papers.

It's just come about as one big mess. I know how much the degree means to her and I'm right behind her decision to do it, but her timing of the summer school is ridiculous. We always go on holiday the last two weeks in June before the prices go up to the peak rates. She knows that. It's the one and only time of the year I get a break. The only time I can properly relax. I work hard enough for it all year, heaven knows. Without these two weeks I reckon I'd crack up.

I'd got it all booked. The flight, the hotel . . . all perfect.

'It might be our last chance for the three of us to have a

holiday together,' I told her. 'Ben will be at college next year and he won't want to come with his parents then.' So what does she do? She goes and books herself into a summer school for the first of those two weeks and says she'll come with us for the second week. How could she do such a thing?

Abbey

(Abbey is staying the weekend with her gran.)

It was so early. I mean really early when I heard this noise outside the bedroom window. A chuckling, cackly sort of a giggle. I knew who it was straight away. I tried to ignore it and go back to sleep. Then there was a crash followed by a louder giggle and I knew I had to get up. I'd promised Mum I'd look after gran and a promise is a promise.

I put my dressing gown on and went outside and there she was. My gran playing frisbee with a load of old vinyl records. She was skimming them up into the air and into her next door neighbour's garden. I didn't know what to do. I just stood and watched, gob-smacked.

She ripped one record out of its purple jacket like there was no tomorrow and she shouts, 'Out you go Frank Sinatra. Out you go. I never liked your crooning. Never!' And she pulled her arm back and flicked the record up high in the air. I could see a thin black whirring shape in the air. Next thing there's a crash and a smashing of glass as the frisbee hits next door's greenhouse.

This is serious, I thought. I took a step towards her. 'Gran?' I said gently. But she didn't hear me. I spoke to her again and reached out to put my hand on her shoulder. But it was as if I wasn't there.

'Take 'em!' she shouted towards the direction of the greenhouse. 'Take all of 'em, Jack,' and she threw all the records up in the air. Jack was my grandad's name and he died when I was a baby.

She walked straight past me as if I didn't exist and back into the house. I just don't know what to do. It's just me and gran alone in the house for the weekend. She's so changed. I used to feel close to her when I lived here all the time. A special sort of love between the two of us you could say. Now I don't know her. She's a stranger doing strange and crazy things and I don't know if I can handle it.

Francine

(Francine is Abbey's mother.)

When they asked me if I minded working the weekends I said, 'No . . . I don't mind'. The truth of it is I could have snatched their hands off. I mean you have to take every chance you can at the moment. Work is work and money is money. I'm just pleased I've got a job.

They pay extra for Sundays and it's such a quiet day. It's a doddle. I'm on reception. It's mainly answering the telephone and nobody seems to want to phone on a Sunday so I settle down and watch the telly in the office. I don't mind it quiet so long as there's something decent to watch.

Abbey and her gran get on so well. Always have. Ever since she was a baby. I think they get on better if I'm out the way. You know what they say . . . 'Two's company and three's a crowd'. I bet they're having a really good time together. Gran hasn't been too well lately . . . but it's nothing serious . . . just old age. Abbey can cope, she's so patient. So . . . we can all enjoy a nice weekend.

Gillian

(Gillian is jealous and planning an act of revenge.)

He's got a new girlfriend. She's not right for him. How could she be? She's so typical. So pretty. I bet she's as boring as hell. I bet she is. I mean she must be.

If you're that good looking you don't have personality. Personality is for ugly cows like me. We need it you see. Some kind of pathetic substitute for beauty. I think she's a complete bitch. I mean she took him.

He thinks she's really nice. It won't last. He'll learn to look deeper. He'll realise that I'm better for him than she is. But it's not his fault. He needed someone and I wasn't there. When he sees I am there, things'll change. I know they will.

I wrote and asked him to meet me. He wrote back to say he was sorry but he couldn't make it. It's complete lies. That bitch told him to write back and say that. He wanted to meet me, but obviously she wouldn't let him.

I know what you're thinking. You think I'm living in a dream world don't you? Well you don't know him and you certainly don't know her. She'd hurt him if it wasn't for me. I know we are going to be back together again soon.

I've chosen the wedding dress. I know he isn't suddenly going to decide tomorrow to give her up. He's waiting for the right moment. He doesn't want to hurt her. He's too nice. But I can wait. My love for him enables me to do that. But of course, I don't have to wait. I mean . . . say something was to happen to her . . . an accident or something like that . . . and I was there for him. But I'll just have to wait . . . maybe . . .

4 *Death*

Jo

(Jo is opposed to fox-hunting.)

I was out walking. It was two weeks ago today. Walking over the fields with a couple of friends from school. We'd crossed over some really muddy fields so we decided to stay on the road for a bit.

We heard some noise on the top of the hill . . . but we couldn't see anything so we just carried on. Then a load of cars came down the road . . . one after another. People in the cars had their windows open and some were looking through binoculars towards the top of the hill. We had to get off the road whilst they drove past.

'It's the hunt,' said Carmel, 'I've seen it out this way before.'

The next thing we knew the hunt was on the road right by us. It was chaos. There were people screaming and shouting, dogs going mad. A fox ran along the road towards us. It was terrified. Then the dogs got to it and killed it. They ripped it to bits. A huntsman on a big grey horse charged at them, beat them back with his whip and picked up what was left of the dead fox and waved it in the air.

I shall never forget that day. Carmel and me have joined the hunt saboteurs. Whatever it takes . . . even if we have to break all the laws in the land . . . we're going to put a stop to fox-hunting.

Joseph

*(Joseph is a native American living in a reservation. The
reservation has a huge wire fence round its perimeter.)*

We live in the reservation. It was built for us many years
ago by the white people. We are very poor and find it
difficult to get work. So we drink and take drugs. When we
do find work it's badly paid and the kind of job nobody else
wants to take.

A few weeks ago there was trouble here. We had a protest
about the way we are treated and there were fights and two
men were killed. As a result of that the white people have
put a big wire fence round the reservation.

'It is to protect you,' they say. 'It will stop any more
trouble.'

But we know different. We are no better than animals in a
cage. We want freedom from white people. We don't want
any part of the white people's way of living. We don't want
to live in cities or to be business people or bankers. We
don't want to drive big cars or to play with technology
gadgets. We want to be ourselves. To be free to fish and
hunt and to bring up our children with our own customs.
We need to live off the land in the ways of our fathers. This
land belonged to us long before the white people came
here.

Some people say our race will not survive and that the death
of our culture has already happened. I believe we will
survive. I will always believe that.

Josh

(Josh is 15.)

Strange, isn't it, how parents try to shield you from
knowing about death? When I was a kid our next door
neighbour died. My mum kept saying that he'd gone away

for a long holiday. It was only ages afterwards that I learned the truth about what had happened when my older sister told me he'd died.

Teachers do the same sometimes. When I was in primary school we had this pet hamster in our class. I used to sit and watch the poor little devil scrabbling about on his wheel in the cage like there was no tomorrow. All day, every day, there he was running round his wheel in his cage. What a life.

The teacher told us the hamster's name was 'Fluff'. Have you ever heard such a stupid name? We didn't call him Fluff. We called him 'Egg Head', 'cos he looked a bit like our head teacher. So whenever she said 'Fluff' all the class went into hysterics and we never let on what we were laughing about.

One day old Egg Head . . . that is the hamster . . . not our head teacher, is lying in his cage with his feet in the air. It's plain for all to see that he has snuffed it. That's what has happened 'cos of all the wheel scrabbling. One kid shouts out, 'Miss . . . the hamster's dead!'

Miss looks up from her sticking bits of painted pasta onto the wall to make a 'flowers of the spring' collage, with a look of horror on her face. She rushes over to open the cage door and I wonder if she's going to give old Egg Head the kiss of life. Now giving a hamster the kiss of life is not an easy task. Miss hesitates and turning her back on us she puts the bundle back in the cage and says, 'Nonsense . . . Fluff is just having a sleep.'

Now we all know that a hamster does not have a sleep with its legs stuck up in the air.

'It is dead Miss,' said a kid sitting next to me. 'Ours looked like that when the cat bit its head off.'

Miss turned on us sharply. 'Now children,' she said, 'I'm just going to take Fluff into the staff room for a change of air . . . but he really is just asleep.'

At dinner time Jason Willy reckoned he saw Miss drive out of the school car park with the hamster's cage in the back of her car. When we get back in the classroom after dinner time there in the usual place is the cage with a hamster scrabbling about on a wheel. Miss proudly announces, 'There we are children, Fluff has woken up from his sleep'. Only this Fluff is much smaller and a slightly different colour and doesn't look a bit like Egg Head and we all know she's done a swap. Bought a new hamster from town. So we all have to pretend Fluff was only asleep.

Kim

(Kim is in hospital after having a near-fatal accident.)

Some details I remember very clearly but other parts are hazy. I go back over it in my mind, again and again, trying to piece it all together so it makes sense.

We were down the shopping centre. Hanging about. There was a group of us having a laugh. There was Craig, Becky, Tim . . . and . . . I can't exactly remember who else . . . We walked past the entrance to the big supermarket like we always did and round the corner to where all the empty shops are. It stinks down there and I wanted to keep going straight through and get to the burger place. Only Tim wanted to stop and read all the graffiti on the boards they put up over the empty shop windows. He reckoned there was something about him on one of them. Craig said, 'As if . . . who would want to write anything about you . . . ?'

But Tim made us stop while he did his ego trip, hoping to see his name in big letters written by some tart who fancied him. Fat chance.

Becky got a bit bored and began to do wheelies on her mountain bike round and round and singing at the top of her voice at the same time. Craig was bored by now as well and reckoned Becky couldn't do wheelies down a load of steps going out onto the car park.

'Want to bet on it?' said Becky.

And the next thing she was doing a giant wheelie right down the steps, brilliant it was.

The next bit is a blur but somehow I know I was on the mountain bike trying to do a wheelie down steps and everybody was laughing. I don't know why they were laughing but even now I can hear them . . . all laughing. I must have fallen off the bike and I think there were some railings at the bottom of the steps. There was the sound of a car as well . . . but it's all mixed up and I still don't know exactly what happened.

Stella

(Stella is a hospital doctor who has been dealing with Kim's accident.)

She is very lucky to be alive. She was unconscious for over 24 hours after the accident and there were injuries to her head and neck. The brain scan did not reveal any bleeding in the skull but that could easily have happened. If that had been the case she might have had more than concussion to cope with.

She is also very stupid. This accident should not have happened. She tries to cycle down a steep flight of steps in some form of stunt to impress her friends and when it all goes wrong we are the ones who have to sort it out. That is irresponsible behaviour of the worst kind. This hospital can barely provide covering services for people who are in need of them. People who bring about their own injuries like this girl should be sent the bill for their stay in hospital. Then, and only then, would they have second thoughts before wasting our time and resources.

Micky

(13 years old.)

It was a Saturday afternoon. Mum was on a late shift and my sister was round her friend's. Me and dad were painting the front room.

I was up the step ladder, dad was mixing up some paint. There was a crash. I turned round. He was lying on the floor in a pool of red paint. I laughed. He'd always been accident prone, my dad. 'Nice one, Dad!' I shouted. He didn't reply. He just lay there.

I sat on top of the ladder and stared at him. I thought, if I stared long enough he'd get up. But he didn't.

I knew I had to do something. Phone me mum. Dial 999. Mouth-to-mouth resuscitation. Something. I knew sitting looking at him wasn't going to solve anything. But I couldn't get down. I couldn't move.

There was a silence like I'd never known before. A cold nothingness. Very still. I was barely breathing. And dad . . .

I wanted him to get up and finish painting the wall. That's all I wanted. It didn't seem much to ask.

It started to get dark. I edged down the ladder. Crept out of the room. I didn't look at the body. I left the house. Walked the streets. Going nowhere. Walking and walking until I knew mum would be home and it'd be safe to go back.

I feel ashamed. Why did I run away? How could I be such a coward?

Chegs

(A teenage football fan.)

This cannot be happening. I thought tragedy went out with Shakespeare. At Christmas we were eighth – within sight of the play-offs.

Then we lost at home to Grimsby. Nobody in their right mind loses at home to Grimsby. And four to one! It had to be a fluke.

Only next week we went to Derby and got turned over three nothing. Four days later, an own goal from our donkey of a centre half sent Barnsley home with a belated Christmas present.

But even then, all was not lost. We were still twelfth. A good run up to Easter. That's all it needed.

Losing at Bognor in the Cup didn't exactly boost confidence.

And then – well, the rest is history. Portsmouth. Sunderland. Millwall. Charlton. You name 'em, we gave 'em the ball and said, 'Here you go, pal, stuff that in the net!'

Things got so dire that when we drew nil-nil with the Wanderers I felt like doing a lap of honour.

I still couldn't believe we'd go down. You can't spend half the season threatening to get promoted and then end up relegated. Most of the points were already in the bag.

Last match of the season. West Brom at home. We only needed the draw. The ninety minutes were up. It was one-one. Surely we were safe now?

IT WAS NOT A PENALTY! NO WAY! I KNOW A PENALTY WHEN I SEE ONE! IT WAS A TRAVESTY OF NATURAL JUSTICE, THAT'S WHAT IT WAS! WHERE IS GOD WHEN YOU NEED HIM?

So – 'Here We Go, Here We Go, Here We Go' . . . into the Second Division. Forced to rub shoulders with Bradford and Rotherham and all sorts of rubbish.

This is the end of the world as we know it.

We might as well be dead.

Chris

(Chris is 16 and is involved in an action group who are attempting to stop the building of a new road in their area.)

The car kills. Not just by causing road accidents. I mean a slow stifling death of strangulation. A death of fumes and stink. A death by metallic paint and flash upholstery, racy motors and car alarms that screech out into the night like some demented creature. It's got a hold on all of us. Its arms reach out in tarmac. Limbs rip out hills and downs, meadows and wildlife of every kind. Where are we hurtling to? Is five minutes off your journey the price we have to pay for a never-ending stream of poison?

But relax. Don't even think about it. Sit easy in the comfort of your reclining seats. Sink forever deeper into the warm foam of your cushions as the earth slowly chokes to death. Earth raper.

Noriko

(On August 6 1945 the atomic bomb was dropped on Hiroshima in Japan. For Noriko living in Hiroshima at the time it was a day that she will never forget.)

On that day, August 6, many of my family and friends died. It was a day that my father did not come home. He did not come home for lunch and I never saw him again.
He had set off very early to work in an office in the city centre. My sister had also left for school and I was alone in the house with my mother. I was just a young child at the time. I remember there was the sound of an air raid siren and my mother switched on the radio. A clear calm voice from the radio said there were three enemy planes heading towards the city. My mother told me it was nothing I should worry about.

A short time later there was a blinding flash of white light. Almost at the same time a huge explosion like a terrible earthquake shook our house. A few seconds later it went dark as if the sun had been put out. Our house began to fall in on top of us.

I don't remember what happened next but somehow my mother must have pulled me out from the rubble of our house and together we staggered towards a river nearby. I will never forget that journey or the sight of the people who staggered along with us. When we reached the river I saw a young girl with pieces of skin hanging from her arms. She was trying to cool herself in the water of the river. As she poured the water on herself more and more of her skin fell away and she cried out in agony.

I try not to remember all I saw and heard that day. But the more I try to forget the more I remember.

Sergei

(Sergei is a scientist who worked on the development of the atomic bomb.)

I feel no shame for what happened at Hiroshima and Nagasaki. It is not for scientists like myself to make decisions about when and where a weapon is used. That is not our job. It is for politicians to make those kind of decisions.

However I do believe that the dropping of the bombs on those cities in Japan shortened the war by several years. In that way our work saved lives rather than destroyed them. Many more people would have been killed in those years of extra fighting than were killed by the atomic bomb.

It has been suggested that we might have dropped a bomb somewhere else first, less populated, to demonstrate the power of an atomic bomb. In this way the Japanese would have seen there was no way they were going to win the war and surrendered immediately. I don't think they would have surrendered. But I don't think that really is my concern. As I said earlier, that is for the politicians to decide not the scientists.

Adrian

(Adrian remembers the death of a reptile.)

I was once shown a rare reptile. It was stunned and in the last throws of its life when it came into my hands. The green scaly skin stretched over its delicate frame. I felt its tiny heart beating inside a trembling rib cage. Its claws splayed and retracted in spasms and its nails scratched over mine creating pain for me when my cuticles tore and began to bleed. Yet my pain was nothing compared to that of this rare creature.

My hands were the reptile's bed and remained motionless as the creature struggled. I stared speechless as the twisting skin and bone created flexed patterns, velvet in texture, and all shades of green.

You know already what is going to happen, so I won't feed it to you in rich language. The lizard died. There you are, my story is complete. It may not have touched you in any way but it touched me and I shared it with you on paper and through the images that it created in your head.

Do you think I could have saved that lizard? Would I have wanted to save its life if I could have? At that time the questions didn't cross my mind as I held its strange body in my hands. We were from two different worlds that lizard and I. Later as I placed its strange body on the cold earth, I knew this reptile, my friend would remain in memory, always.

5 *Death Row*

Esmonde

(Esmonde is 24 years old and has lived in the United States since he was ten. Four years ago he killed a shop keeper and was sentenced to die by lethal injection. Since then he has been waiting on Death Row.)

They can't do this to me.

I'm a British subject. I deserve British justice.

I never killed Mr Schwitzer on purpose. It was his fault. He came at me with a bat. I warned him. I said, 'Get back, this is a real gun, it's not a replica'. But he wouldn't listen. What else could I do? I only meant to wound him. If I hadn't fired he'd've beaten me to death wouldn't he?

I only wanted the money, that's all. I didn't want to kill no one. Self protection, that's all it was.

I was only 19 when it happened. We all make mistakes. Killing me won't bring back Mr Schwitzer will it?

I don't want to die. They got no right. I'm not an American citizen.

I don't want to die.

Sherry

(41, Esmonde's mother.)

He was a good lad. He always did as he was told . . .

I wish that was true. But the truth is Esmonde was always trouble. When he was seven he got expelled from school for beating up younger kids. I don't know why he's like he is. There's an anger inside him. There always has been. He's just like his father.

When I remarried and moved to the States I thought about leaving Esmonde behind. But it was obvious his dad wasn't interested in looking after him. Charlie, my new husband, said maybe all the lad needed was a fresh start. Charlie thinks the best of everyone. He soon changed his tune, though. Within weeks of coming over Esmonde was running riot again. By sixteen he'd dropped out of school. He can't control himself. Most of us have an in-built sensor in our heads that tells us we're overstepping the mark. But not Esmonde. Half the time he doesn't even see what he's doing. When he was eighteen there was talk of him being deported to England. Charlie and I fought tooth and nail to keep him with us. I wish we hadn't bothered . . . .

In the end even patient Charlie had enough. One day he caught Esmonde stealing my jewellery and threw him out of the house. Esmonde broke down in tears, like a little kid. It used to break my heart to see him cry. But this time I knew that pity was useless. Esmonde has never cared about anyone but himself. Love is wasted on him. The truth is, he'll be better off out of this world.

Marissa

(Esmonde's defence attorney.)

I met Esmonde three years ago. He's clearly a very disturbed young man. He's deeply paranoid. He is one of the few people I've met who doesn't seem to have a capacity for compassion. On several occasions he's threatened me with violence when an appeal went against him.

So why do I fight to save him from the death chamber? The answer's simple. I believe in justice. I believe that justice is about doing what you know to be morally correct.

That Esmonde murdered George Schwitzer is not in dispute. Nor would anyone argue that he is ever likely to be rehabilitated into society. But that does not justify the taking of his life. If we believe in a moral code we must be prepared to accept some responsibility when that code breaks down.

You see, there's an inconsistency here. We say killing people is wrong, barbaric, inhuman. But then we say that because murder is such a heinous crime it must be punished with a death sentence. We want it both ways.

We live in a post-industrial technological age and our response to wrongdoing is straight out of the Old Testament. An eye for an eye. A life for a life. Revenge is not justice. Execution is not justice.

Execution is murder. Period.

Drewer

(A campaigner for 'Families Against Evil'.)

Esmonde Willis walked into George Schwitzer's drug store. He demanded money. When he didn't get it he shot the guy dead. George Schwitzer was forty-two years old. He had three children. His wife, Mary-Ellen, was expecting their fourth. Willis destroyed six lives. There was less than two hundred dollars in the till.

Are you gonna tell me that's defensible? Are you gonna say the schmuck had a bad childhood and his Mom hated him and he was no good at math so that makes him some kinda special case? Get outta here.

Until we see things for what they are, nothing's gonna change.

I want my family to live in a society where you can drive down the street and not have to keep a gun under your seat. I want to walk through shopping malls and not have to worry that the guy coming toward me might be a psycho. I want the murderous scum where they belong. Six feet under, pushing up daisies.

There is right and there is wrong. There is good and there is evil. God gave us the gift of free will. We make our decisions and we pay the price.

I want to see Esmonde Willis pay for the evil he has done. If I had my way it wouldn't be no lethal injection. He oughta be hanged, real slow, so that he feels something of the suffering he's inflicted on others.

Mary-Ellen

(George Schwitzer's widow.)

Esmonde Willis killed my husband. He left my children with no father. We have to live with our loss for the rest of our lives.

All I ask is that justice be done, that Willis receive the maximum sentence possible.

When the jury passed the death sentence, something inside me, a kind of gut feeling that I can't describe, said 'No!'

Death is not the solution.

Life imprisonment without parole. That's the maximum sentence. That's what Esmonde Willis deserves.

6 *Monologues in Action*

1 *For discussion*
Do you think Beth is accurately describing Terry's behaviour?
What might be the reasons for this behaviour?

2 *Try this game*
Terry is in his twenties when he becomes a dad. Explore his past
life, and the fact that he had two dads, with a drama game. All
sit round in a big circle and number yourselves consecutively
beginning at number one. The teacher then calls a number at
random and the person with that number is invited to give a
statement relating to Terry at that age. As you build up the
statements a picture of Terry should emerge. Listen to each
other and make your statements so they give a *believable* picture
of Terry. Avoid ideas that would be too comic or unrealistic.

3 *Still images*
Explore the key moments in Terry's life as you have shown it in
the game by creating a series of still images. Work in small
groups. You can then bring the images to life for a few seconds
adding dialogue or narration.

4 *The future*
Think about the future for Terry, Beth and their baby. Choose
any moment in this future, days, weeks, months or years later, as
you imagine it might be. Sit round in the circle again and work
your way round with each person stating a particular time and a
brief description of what might be happening to the family at
that time.

GEMMA	*page 2*
EMMA	*page 3*

1   In order to explore the different attitudes involved in this situation you will need to represent the roles of the two girls. Working as a full class sit in one big circle, facing *outwards*. Go round the circle with each person having the opportunity to say a thought as if they were Emma. Remember you are *representing* Emma so you can speak in your own voice trying to be truthful to her character. Once this has been achieved turn *inwards* in the circle and repeat the process only this time giving the thoughts of Gemma.

2   *Forum Theatre*
Imagine the two are to meet. Emma is coming round to Gemma's house in order to talk over their difficulties. How should she approach this task? Working in small groups discuss how she should handle the meeting. What should she say? How should she react?
Once the groups have discussed this, ask one of your class to take the role of Emma. Each group in turn should then give her the advice they have agreed upon.
Now set up the meeting in Gemma's house. Place a few objects to suggest the room they are to meet in. Ask one of your class to take the role of Gemma and let the scene run. You can stop the action any time you wish, taking 'time out', to give either role further advice so they can come to a resolution of their difficulties. You can also swap over the roles, allowing a number of the class to participate in the scene in turn. But remember, you need to work towards a positive outcome to the scene.

3   You might need to talk to Greg, who Gemma mentions in her monologue. Ask one of your class to take his role whilst the rest 'hot seat' him in order to find out more about this religious sect. As an alternative perhaps your teacher could take this role in the hot seating activity.

ERNA	*page 3*

1   *For discussion*
How do you feel about Erna's plight? Why do you think the woman who helped with the delivery of Erna's baby disappeared? What might have happened to her?

2   *Monologue writing*
    Choose one fictional character of your own who lived during the
    time of the Second World War. This might be someone who lost
    their home in Britain due to bombing, a soldier on home leave
    or in the midst of the fighting, a woman working in the factories
    or a young evacuee. Write a monologue telling of their
    experiences in the war. You might need to focus upon one
    particular moment in time when a crisis faces them.

3   *Group work*
    Work in small groups and read out your monologues to each
    other. What do the monologues add to your understanding of
    the Second World War in general?

4   Using the monologues you have written devise your own scene
    based on the characters you have created. You may wish to use
    some of your writing or Erna's monologue as a basis for a script
    for the scene. You might need to introduce additional characters
    in your scene.

GRACE   *page 4*

1   In her monologue Grace remembers a childhood experience of
    visiting the 'family house' and her first sights of the new baby.
    Read the monologue again taking note of any particular
    descriptions which strike you. Now turn to a partner and share
    your responses to the monologue with them.

2   *Storytelling*
    Find a space for yourself and think back over any childhood
    experiences that come to mind. These experiences might include
    babies or houses you have lived in or visited. Choose one
    experience you will feel comfortable in sharing with someone
    else. Work on the details of the experience and begin to build a
    short story or description which you can share with your partner.
    What strikes you most about the experience? What visual
    pictures do you remember? How did you feel at the time? Think
    carefully about how you will begin your story. You will need to
    capture your partner's attention throughout.

3   *Pair work*
    Find some space for you and your partner to tell your stories to
    each other. Decide who is to tell their story first. Try to listen
    attentively as your partner tells their story and don't interrupt

them. Ask a few sensitive questions if they 'dry up'. After the story is told feed back your response to them, saying which parts of the story or the telling most interested you.

4   *Audiences*
You have just told your story to an audience of one. Working now as a full group, and hearing some of the stories again, begin to list the skills you need to have when you are storytelling. These may be the same skills you need when you are in a drama performance. Discuss the skills which are needed when you perform in plays and in storytelling.

CRYSTAL   *page 5*

1   *Forming a character/hot seating*
Taking Crystal's monologue as a starting point try to build a picture of what you think Ryan might be like when he's five years old.
To help do this you might want to hot seat Crystal and get her view on his personality and character.

2   *The life of Ryan*
A free flowing whole group improvisation.
The aim is to act out the life of Ryan, from early childhood to adolescence, adulthood and beyond.
Select one member of the group to role play Ryan, who will act as the opening narrator for this improvised story. The narrator leads the drama by introducing scenes from his life – e.g. 'I remember when I was three years old my mum turned to me and said . . .' and other members of the group make up impromptu scenes from Ryan's life.
Spontaneity is the secret to this impro game. Try to allow Ryan's character and story to build through action rather than discussion. As the drama progresses other group members might have an idea of what could happen next and will want to take over the narration. Let them!

3   *Group discussion*
At the end of the improvisation discuss the decisions that you have collectively made about Ryan's life. What kind of a life have you given him? How has he developed as a character? To what extent are the events of his life based upon your early character-building exercise?

4   Think of your own lives to date. Do you feel you were born with
a unique personality which governs your behaviour, or is your
character shaped by the circumstances of your life – e.g. where
you live, who you know, the chances you get, the attitudes of
other people around you.
Which theory – nature or nurture – does your 'Life of Ryan'
drama seem to support, if any?

DOM	*page 6*
LARA	*page 6*
MR HARDY	*page 7*

1   *Devising scenes*
Divide into groups and ask each group to devise a different
scene based on Dom's life as a DJ. Try to include all the
characters from the monologues and show their contrasting
feelings and attitudes to what is taking place. You might wish to
include scenes between Dom and his father or when Dom meets
Lara.

2   *Presentation*
Once you've rehearsed the scenes begin to plan the best way to
present them as a whole story. Think about the order of the
scenes, the use of music and props. Are you able to include any
visual effects?

3   Once you've presented the scenes begin to think about Dom's
future. He says, 'It's all there waiting for me'. Do you think his
view is a realistic one? Devise one final scene as a whole group or
in small groups depicting the future for Dom as you imagine it
to be.

HENRY STONE	*page 8*
ALICE	*page 9*
HOWARD COYNE	*page 10*
TED WEAVER	*page 10*
MARJORIE	*page 11*

1   *Titanic* was a huge ship, 'the largest man-made moving object
which had ever been built'. For example, the vessel was almost
900 feet long. In order to have some distinct sense of this size

use a large space outside to pace out the length of the ship. You might need to use markers to help you with this task. Stand back and have a look at this size and try to visualise details of the appearance of the ship. Library research would provide you with further evidence and details.

2   Henry Stone's monologue gives us some information regarding the sea trials of the ship. Imagine you are travelling on board *Titanic* during the trials or during the maiden voyage. Write entries in a diary seen from the view point of your imaginary passenger. You could then dramatise these using extracts from the diary as your narration.

3   *Interviews*
Working in pairs and using the monologue of Alice as your starting point set up an interview of a survivor from *Titanic*. Your interview could be in 1912 or many years later when the objects and personal belongings from the wreck have been put on public display.

4   *Conscience Alley*
Read the monologues of Howard Coyne, Ted Weaver and Marjorie in order to have a clear picture about the morality of raising personal belongings from the wreck. Now ask one of your class to represent Howard Coyne and set up a conscience alley in order to test if further visits to the wreck involving the raising of belongings should be undertaken. His future action should depend on the power of your persuasion. For details of how to set up the conscience alley see page 51 of this book.

LOKIATH	*page 12*
MASLOV	*page 12*

1   What Lokiath has seen pressed into the snow is a huge creature's footprint. Talk about what the footprint might look like and, using chalk, tape, or rope, create the outline of the footprint.

2   Look at the shape and imagine it is the creature's footprint. Take on the role of the villagers in Lokiath's village and create a still image of the moment the footprint has been discovered. Now bring the moment to life with everyone staying in role.

3   Set up a meeting to decide what action has to be taken. Your teacher might take the role of Maslov and 'chair' the meeting.

4   Depending on what is decided, shape the rest of the drama using
    still images, small group work, and devised scenes to tell the
    story of this seemingly cursed race of people.

RAVI	*page 13*
SIMON	*page 14*

1   The teacher divides the class into two random halves. One half
    of the group now take the roles of the local people who live near
    the dam whilst the other half of the group take the roles of those
    building the dam. Working in the two groups consider the
    events leading up to the dam protest. These events might
    include the times when local people are moved away from their
    homes, the early work on the dam, discussion in the nearby
    villages of the impact of the dam. Once you've decided on a
    couple of these events decide on the most appropriate way to
    perform them. You might decide to use devised scenes, still
    images, narration, mime or storytelling. Prepare your
    performances and then show them to the other half of the class.
    Discuss the different interpretations of the events that the two
    groups have given.

2   Work now as one group and set up the actual protest. Use
    objects in your room to represent the dam, etc. You'll need to
    make one full class still image at the height of the protest. The
    teacher organises 'thought tracking' in which each person in the
    still image is asked to verbalise their thoughts 'in role' as the
    teacher taps them on the shoulder.

3   All the class now take different roles – those of a peace keeping
    task force who should work to resolve the problems encountered
    by the two groups. You may need to interview Ravi or Simon
    (individuals in role). Have small discussion groups as you work
    towards a plan of action. Agree your full action plan and show
    how successful you think it will be by creating one final full class
    still image to show the future of the project.

MICHAEL	*page 15*
JOANNA	*page 16*

1   *For discussion*
    How serious a situation do you think this is? Is Joanna right not
    to want to make a fuss?

2   *Hot seating*
Split the class into two groups. Each group acts as counsellors for one of the characters. Focus on the incident in the dining hall when Michael brushes against Joanna.
Group A: discuss with Michael why he is so in love with Joanna and what he plans to do about his obsession. Is he aware of how threatening his behaviour is?
Group B: discuss with Joanna why she is reluctant to 'make a fuss'. Has this kind of incident happened before? Do you think she should report the incident?

3   *Forum Theatre*
Forum Theatre is a role play activity where two or more people act out a scene in front of the rest of the group. At any time an observer can shout 'Stop!' and suggest an action for one or other of the characters that might help resolve the scene.
Set up the following situation: Joanna is walking home through the park. Michael is following her at a distance. Joanna's objective in this scene is to confront Michael and get him to leave her alone. Michael's objective is to ask her out – he's worked himself up to this moment, he's determined to declare his love.
Try the scene over several times with different character responses. For instance, what happens if Joanna tries to be polite and not hurt Michael's feelings, or if she loses her temper and tells him to leave her alone?
You can introduce other characters to the scene to help resolve the situation – e.g. Joanna's friends, a teacher, Trevor, a passer-by etc.

PAT   *page 16*

1   *For discussion*
We learn very little about Pat or Sam in this monologue. As a whole group discuss what kind of people you think they might be. How long do you think they've known each other? Why do you think 'everyone is making such a fuss'? Why do Sam's parents want to drive them apart?

2   *Hot seating*
To help answer this last question you might hot seat Sam's parents. Select two group members to role play the parents and allow them a few minutes on their own to discuss their characters.

You could extend this activity by introducing other characters who know Sam and Pat and have an opinion about their relationship.

3   *Word association*
Love is a big, encompassing word. In small groups create a flow chart of the different meanings you think this word can have. Start by writing 'Love' in the centre of a large piece of paper and add other words that you feel connect with the word 'Love'.

4   Using the chart you've created, how would you define Pat and Sam's love?

'ROMEO'	*page 17*
'JULIET'	*page 18*

1   *For discussion*
Read the two monologues and consider the following questions:
  i   Do you agree with Romeo and Juliet's decision to adopt false names and keep their relationship a secret?
  ii Why do you think Juliet's parents want her to marry Rashid?
  iii How realistic is Romeo's plan to run away?
  iv Juliet states, 'There must be another way of sorting things out'. What alternatives can you think of?

2   *Acting out*
Set up and develop the following scenes to explore the ideas raised in the monologues:
  i   Juliet in the newsagent. It's busy and Romeo's dad is ignoring her and serving people behind her in the queue.
  ii Romeo has been seen with Juliet. His parents want to know who she is and what they were doing together.
  iii Act out the same scenario for Juliet and her parents.

3   *Crisis point*
At the end of his monologue Romeo is at the hideaway, waiting for Juliet to arrive so that they can run away. Using the ideas you've developed in discussion and in the earlier acted-out scenes, show what happens when Juliet arrives.
Make this scene the crisis point for both characters – i.e. the conclusion they reach will have a lasting effect on their relationship.

JULIE

1   *Creating a character*
    Split the class into three groups. Each group is given a character
    to develop – Julie, Steve or Nick. Take turns to contribute one
    'fact' about the character you are creating, making sure that each
    new fact builds on what has already been said.

2   *Discussion*
    Having drawn up an identity for each character, share your ideas
    with the rest of the class and discuss the range of characters you
    have created. Read Julie's monologue again and discuss the
    picture you now have of her relationship with Nick.

3   *Acting out*
    In pairs act out a scene where Julie returns from her night with
    Steve to find that Nick has arrived home early.

4   *The future*
    What kind of future do you see for Julie and Nick? You can
    explore this through discussion, acting out further scenes set in
    the future, or by writing your own monologues showing the
    points of view of Julie, Steve and Nick.

MOLLY

1   *For discussion*
    How do you feel about Molly's problems? What advice would
    you give her?

2   *Hot seating*
    Working as a whole class decide on who would be the most
    interesting people to meet who could give you more
    information about Molly. When you have done this, see if
    anyone in your class might be prepared to take on the role of
    any of these. If they take a role, the rest of the class should ask
    them relevant questions which they answer in role. Your
    questions should not try to trick the person taking the role but
    should seek out attitudes and feelings towards Molly.

3   *Conscience Alley*
    Molly may be thinking of leaving her husband. Set up a
    conscience alley to explore moments of her decision making.
    The class does this by standing in two lines facing each other.
    One of the class takes the role of Molly and walks very *slowly*

down the line, whilst the rest take it in turns to give her advice
as she passes. One line should give reasons why she should
continue with the marriage, whilst the other gives opposing
reasons to end the marriage. At the end of this your 'Molly'
should make a decision based upon the advice given.

4   *Your own monologues*
Think about the people who might be involved with Molly. Her
parents, friends, family and husband could be included in your
list. Write a monologue from their perspective about the
problems Molly faces. You can write these by yourself or in pairs.
When they are complete, read them out to the rest of the class
and discuss how they further your understanding of the
situation.

LYDIA	*page 21*
. **ROBBIE**	*page 21*

1   Examine the attitudes of Lydia and Robbie. Why do you think
they have such different views of the first time they slept
together?

2   *Debate*
Set up a class debate on the following resolution:
'Making love is a decision that two people make for themselves.
Everyone else should mind their own business.'
What rules do you feel should govern teenage sex? What are the
dangers? What are the positive aspects? Is it always important in
a relationship?
You could develop this activity by getting members of the group
to role play characters representing different interests – e.g. a
devout Christian, a protective parent, a health-care worker etc.

BEN	*page 22*
TIM	*page 23*

1   *Solo work*
We do not have a first-hand account from Ben's mother in these
monologues and in order to build more details about her, your
help is invited. Find a space by yourself and then:
a   Read both monologues again to have a clearer picture about
the relationships which are involved.
b   Give Ben's mother a first name and decide a few details about

her personality and appearance. How might she be dressed? Try to imagine as many details as you can and then share your ideas with the rest of the class. How many ideas were similar?

2 *Pair work*
In order to explore the relationship between Ben and his mother or father devise a scene between them. This might be when the problem over the holiday is discussed.

3 *Forum Theatre*
Working as a whole class look at problematic moments of interaction between Ben's mother and father. Take 'time out' giving the characters advice as to how they should overcome their problems and rerun the interactions. For further details of how to organise the forum theatre see the action work for 'Gemma' and 'Emma'.

ABBEY	*page 24*
FRANCINE	*page 25*

1 *Try this game*
Everybody sits in a circle. Each person thinks of an object that might belong to Abbey's Gran which has had some significance in Gran's past life. It might be a photograph, an old coin, an old post card etc. Go half way round the circle and hear what each member of your class has chosen. After you have done this pause for some reflection.
How many people chose similar objects? What do the objects tell you about Gran's past life?
Now continue round the circle, only this time each person creates a very short story or description to introduce their choice of object – 'This postcard is from Italy. It was the very first time Gran went abroad for her holidays', etc.

2 *Pair work*
Using the objects and the stories offered in the game as a starting point devise a short scene based on an episode in Gran's past life.

3 *Abbey's dilemma*
The previous activities explored the past. Abbey now has a problem of coping with Gran over the weekend.
What should she do? Working in small groups talk over what advice you would give Abbey. When you have done this ask for a

volunteer to take the role of Abbey. Place your 'Abbey' in the centre of the circle and ask each group to give their advice in turn to her. Once this has been given ask Abbey to give her thoughts as to her future actions.

4   *A final activity*
Look into the future as you see it for Abbey, her Gran, and Francine. Working in small groups create a still image which expresses your future picture.

GILLIAN   *page 26*

1   *Creating an environment*
Consider where Gillian is when we hear her monologue. Working in small groups create this space by placing a few simple objects to represent the space and things within the space. By placing a chair, for example, you might indicate a CD player in Gillian's bedroom, or a desk might suggest a table in a cafe where she is sitting.
What more do we learn about Gillian now?

2   *The letter*
The monologue mentions a letter she received. Decide upon a few details about the person who sent it, and then write the letter.

3   *Pair work*
Consider the moment Gillian receives the letter. Use the environments you have created and the letters. One of you takes the role of Gillian. The other member of the pair takes the task of director and directs the scene using a part, or all of the text of the monologue, and the letter.

4   *The future*
Imagine what the future holds for Gillian and the two people she talks about. Working in small groups create a series of still images to show key moments in this future. You can then add a spoken narration to link the images together.

JO   *page 27*

1   *Research*
Find out more about animal rights and animal rights organisations. Collect articles from newspapers and magazines. Invite visitors into your school who might give you different,

and balancing, opinions about the subject.

2   *Organise a debate about animal rights*
    Decide upon a particular motion to debate and ask for
    volunteers to represent either side of the argument. Hear their
    case, ask questions and take a final vote.

3   *A court room drama*
    Jo says that she is prepared to 'break all the laws in the land' to
    stop fox-hunting. Imagine an incident that happens when Jo
    does this, and as a result a court case is brought. Decide what
    the incident is and set up your classroom as a court room. You
    will need to hear evidence from several people. Your verdict can
    be determined by a jury or by a whole class vote.

JOSEPH   *page 28*

1   Take two large pieces of paper and draw a rough outline of the
    character of Joseph on each. Working in two groups write
    suitable words or phrases inside the outlines which express
    characteristics of Joseph. One of the groups should write from
    Joseph's own point of view, the other from the white people's.
    Placing the two sheets side by side, discuss the comments you
    have written.

2   Ask a member of the class to take the role of Joseph. Perhaps
    this could be your teacher. The rest of the group are in role as
    advisers trying to help Joseph. By a process of hot seating try to
    find out what Joseph is feeling and fearing. Then try to agree
    about what should be done for Joseph and his people.

3   Make a large circle of chairs to depict the reservation within
    which the American Indians live. Place everybody inside the
    circle and ask them to take up a still position in role as American
    Indians. Their positions should express their emotions and
    feelings. Speaking in turn use one word or a phrase to say what
    you are thinking.

4   Research the heritage of the American Indian. How do you
    think they have been treated? What might the future hold for
    them?

JOSH   *page 28*

1   *For discussion*
     Look at Josh's first sentence about parents shielding the truth
     from young people. Do you think they do? Are there times
     when this is:
     a   essential?
     b   unwise?

2   *Monologue writing*
     Josh's account of the incident with the dead hamster is only one
     version of what happened. Write a monologue from the
     viewpoint of the teacher regarding this incident. Read the
     monologues to each other and discuss how their versions of
     what happened vary from Josh's.

3   *Breaking bad news*
     Breaking bad news is never an easy task. Working in pairs devise
     two scenes where each of you has to give bad news to the other.
     Remember these are fictional scenes so the bad news can be
     whatever you decide. Try to make the scenes convincing and
     realistic and when you've completed them chat over the most
     appropriate ways to approach this difficult task.

KIM   *page 30*

STELLA   *page 31*

1   *For discussion*
     Stella says that Kim's accident is 'irresponsible behaviour of the
     worst kind'. Do you agree with her? How do you feel about her
     remark that 'People who bring about their own injuries like this
     girl should be sent the bill for their stay in hospital'?

2   *Posters*
     Think about creating a poster which would warn people about
     the dangers of cycling. Work in small groups and create a poster
     by forming a dramatic still image which should have an impact
     upon those who see it.

3   *Captions*
     Share the image you have created with the rest of the class. Ask
     your audience to consider the essence of your image/poster by
     offering a suitable caption.

4   Once your images and captions have been offered re-read the

monologues of Kim and Stella. Now compose two new captions for each image to express their contrasting attitudes. How do the new captions change your response to the images?

MICKY   *page 32*

1   *Pairs work*
    Divide into pairs. One person plays the role of Micky, the other Micky's friend. Micky feels very guilty about the way he reacted to his father's death. What advice can his friend offer to help him make sense of his reaction?

2   *Group or solo work*
    Think of a time when you have responded to a situation in a way that you later regretted. The incident you choose may be important or trivial. Describe why you behaved as you did, and how you would react if the same thing happened again.
    This exercise can be undertaken either as a whole group discussion or as an individual writing project.

3   *A new beginning*
    The death of a loved one is one of the hardest things to accept and understand. Often, people can't communicate their grief, even to those close to them. Develop a short play depicting life for Micky, his mother, and his sister, in the months following his father's death. How do they cope with their grief and build a new life for themselves? Is it possible for them to come to terms with what has happened and still preserve their memories?

CHEGS   *page 33*

A video project
Take the monologue as a starting point for making your own video about football. What impression of football do you have after reading Chegs's monologue? How typical is he of a football fan?
After discussing your response begin to plan your own video. The following guidelines should help you:

1   Think of the style of video you wish to make. Is it to be a documentary, a 'teenage diary', a video with an original angle, a day in the life of a player or a fan? Could it be about a women's football team?

2   Plan carefully before you begin filming. Working in a group is important. Share responsibilities and decision making.

3   Practice using the video camera, playing back what you've recorded. Experiment with camera angles, try different locations, and become familiar with the equipment before you begin recording your final video.

4   Use a Story Board to plan your work. Draw rough sketches in picture frames to provide details of the sequences of the main parts of the video.

5   If you're using a presenter, write a script for the commentary. Think about ways of varying the narration, using voice-over and direct-to-camera address.

6   Share your planning ideas with the rest of the class. You can use 'freeze frame' drama and narration to present your ideas. Ask the class to give you feedback.

7   If you wish to use outside locations check they are available and that your recording does not cause inconvenience to others.

8   Be realistic about what you can achieve. A video lasting no more than ten minutes in a finished state should be the maximum to aim for.

CHRIS *page 34*

1   *Hot seating*
    Ask one of your class to take the role of Chris whilst the rest ask questions concerning Chris's feelings and beliefs.

2   *An opposite point of view*
    Try to think of a number of different characters who would give an opposite point of view to that given by Chris. Try not to stereotype these characters but be able to offer a point of view with which you might have some sympathy.

3   *Monologue writing*
    From the characters you have chosen select one who most interests you and write a monologue expressing their point of view.

4   *Devising scenes*
    Work in groups of three. One of the characters in your group is Chris, the second is one of the characters created in the

monologues, the third is someone trying to make a choice between the conflicting viewpoints. Your devised scene should explore the dilemma faced by the third person.

NORIKO	*page 34*
SERGEI	*page 35*

1   *Interviews*
    Work in pairs. One of you takes the role of Sergei and the other acts as a TV or radio interviewer. The person playing Sergei should read the monologue through carefully as preparation for this whilst the interviewer thinks of a number of questions to ask. You could record your interviews on audio tape or video if you have these facilities available.

2   *Whole group work*
    Set up the room you are working in to represent part of the city of Hiroshima moments before the atomic bomb was dropped. Do this by placing chairs etc. to suggest buildings and open spaces. Look at the space you have created and discuss the impression of Hiroshima it gives you. All the class now take up still positions in the space as people of the city. The teacher walks round the space and as she approaches a particular part the people begin to speak and move until the teacher then moves off to a different part of the room.

3   *Aftermath*
    Out of role rearrange your room *carefully* to represent the city after the bomb has been dropped and then create new still images in the space. As the teacher moves round the room this time you can move if you wish to and add the words spoken by Sergei either in the monologue or in the interview. What impact do these words have?

ADRIAN	*page 36*

1   *For discussion*
    Why do you think this incident has remained in Adrian's memory? How would you describe the feelings which are expressed in the monologue?

2   *Solo work*
    Find a space by yourself and think over times you have had strange or disturbing experiences with an animal. This might be

when a pet died or was injured, when you were frightened by an animal, or if you saw an animal killed. Try to remember how you felt at the time.

3 *Pair work*
Share your account with a partner and then chat about the feelings you have both expressed. What were the differences and similarities?

4 *Dramatisation*
Using extracts from your accounts as narration, create a short dramatisation of these episodes. Think carefully about the most appropriate style of dramatisation to choose. You might wish to use mime, dance drama, linked images and narration, slow motion, or music. What is important is that you explore the feelings of your experiences.

ESMONDE	*page 38*
SHERRY	*page 38*
MARISSA	*page 39*
DREWER	*page 40*
MARY-ELLEN	*page 41*

1 *Reading the monologues*
Select five members of the group to read the monologues. Allow them some preparation time before they read their part. Place each character in their own space, so that they cannot hear or react to what anyone else is saying. Present the monologues in the order they are laid out – i.e. Esmonde, Sherry, Marissa, Drewer, Mary-Ellen. After you've heard all the characters, decide which – if any – you most readily identify with. Did your sympathies change at all during the sequence? Do you feel the order of the monologues influences the way you respond to them?

2 *Character work – role play*
Divide the class into five groups. Each group takes a character to analyse. Begin by identifying the overriding attitude of your character – what is it that motivates them to say what they say? Develop a short scene that you feel gives a clear picture of what the character is like. This could involve developing an incident mentioned in the monologue or inventing an experience from the character's past that had a profound effect on their thinking.

3   Take turns to present your scene to the rest of the class.
The object of this exercise is not to decide whether a character's
attitude is right or wrong, but to explain the rationale behind
their thinking.

4   *'People's Forum' television debate*
Create a television chat show that is going to debate capital
punishment. The title of the debate is 'Esmonde Willis: Should
He Die?'
Allow a strict time limit for the programme (e.g. 30 minutes).
The aim is to listen to all the arguments and at the end to decide
what the 'will of the people' is by taking a poll of the audience.
Allow plenty of time to plan and prepare for the debate. Begin
by allocating roles. You'll need:
A host. This is a crucial role. The host will need to control the
debate, remain impartial, and ensure that everyone has a chance
to put their point across. You might want to have more than one
host. It might also be a good idea to have a 'team' to help devise
the questions the host is going to ask.
A panel of guests. This will probably include most of the
characters with monologues but can also include other
representatives, e.g. the police, the church, other victims of
crime, reformed ex-cons etc. Try to work out which, if any, of
the panellists are likely to be in agreement with each other and
might benefit from planning their arguments together.
The studio audience. If you already have a very clear opinion
about capital punishment you might prefer to be a member of
the audience. This will enable you to voice your own views
rather than having to adopt a fictitious character's perspective.
NB   When choosing the characters for the TV forum, bear in
mind that Esmonde is in jail and therefore unable to be in the
studio.